# Story Cake

## By Joy Cowley

### Illustrated by Patricia Ludlow

Dominie Press, Inc.

Publisher: Christine Yuen
Editor: John S. F. Graham
Designer: Lois Stanfield
Illustrator: Patricia Ludlow

Published by:

🍃 **Dominie Press, Inc.**

1949 Kellogg Avenue
Carlsbad, California 92008 USA

www.dominie.com

Paperback ISBN 0-7685-1065-1
Library Bound Edition ISBN 0-7685-1490-8
Printed in Singapore by PH Productions Pte Ltd
   2 3 4 5 6 PH 04 03

# Table of Contents

## Chapter One

# We Are Hungry for Stories

Carlos and Rosa
went to Mrs. Bueno,
the story cake maker.

"Mrs. Bueno!" called Carlos.
"We want a story cake."

"I am busy," said Mrs. Bueno.
"I am sewing sleepy songs
for a lullaby quilt."

"Please, Mrs. Bueno," said Rosa.
"We are hungry for stories."

"You make the best story cakes
in the world," Carlos said.

Mrs. Bueno put down her sewing.
"What kind of story cake
do you want?" she asked.

"An adventure story!" cried Rosa.

## Chapter Two

# The Recipe

**M**rs. Bueno put a big bowl
on her counter.

Into the big bowl
she put an interesting place.

Into that interesting place
she put two characters,
a girl called Rosa
and a boy called Carlos.

Next, she opened a jar
that held all kinds of villains,
some big and some small.
Mrs. Bueno chose a small, greedy villain
and put him into the bowl.

"You need a friend," said Mrs. Bueno,
and she put in a friend.

"You need a little danger," she said.
In went a spoonful of danger.

"Oh," said Mrs. Bueno.
"I nearly forgot. We need worry,
but also a happy ending."
She put in a cupful of happy ending,
then she stirred and stirred.

Chapter Three

# An Oven Called Imagination

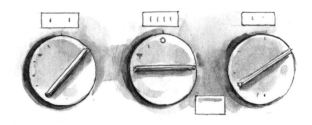

**W**hile Carlos and Rosa watched,
Mrs. Bueno put the story cake
into the oven, which had a name.
The oven was called *Imagination.*
Mrs. Bueno smiled and said,
"All my story ovens
have been called *Imagination.*"

The adventure cake was ready
in about five small blinks.
It looked delicious.

Carlos and Rosa couldn't wait
for the cake to cool.
They broke it in half,
tossed it in their fingers,
and nibbled it hot.

Chapter Four

# The Eagle

Carlos and Rosa
found themselves
on a wild, steep mountain.
They were carrying a box of gold
home to their mother.

Below them, far, far away,
was the river.
Above them, high in the sky,
flew an eagle.

Carlos and Rosa stopped
to have some lunch.
They put the box of gold
down on the path,
and ate their bread.

"Caw! Caw!" cried the eagle.

"Poor eagle! It's hungry!"
said Carlos, and he and Rosa
gave the eagle some bread.

"Caw!" said the eagle,
in a happy voice.

## Chapter Five

# The Greedy Gold Grabber

Carlos and Rosa did not know
that there was a villain
creeping up on them.
It was the Greedy Gold Grabber,
with *GGG* on his T-shirt.

While the children were eating,
the Greedy Gold Grabber
rushed up with twitchy fingers
and grabbed the box of gold.
Then he ran back along the path.
"My gold!" he shouted. "All mine!"

Carlos and Rosa tried to run
after the greedy villain,
but the path was narrow
and dangerous.

"Help!" Carlos cried.

The eagle heard.
It swooped down,
flapping its wings.

The Greedy Gold Grabber
got such a fright
that he dropped the box of gold
over the edge of the cliff.

Down, down, went the box,
down to the river.

The eagle went after it.

Just as the box hit the water,
the eagle pounced on it.

"Saved!" cried Carlos.

"What a happy ending!" said Rosa.

## Chapter Six

# Crumbs

**R**osa brushed the crumbs
of story cake off her jeans.
"That was a delicious adventure,"
she said to Mrs. Bueno.

Mrs. Bueno picked up her quilt.
"All good adventure stories
must come to an end," she said.
"Now it is time for me
to do my sewing."

Rosa and Carlos stood up.

Mrs. Bueno smiled.
"If you want another story,
read a book," she told them.
"Books have lots of adventures."